NUMBER TWO POO-POO

POOP

SCAT

FECES

POOP
Eaters

STOOL

by Ellen Lawrence

Consultant:
Garret Suen, Assistant Professor
Department of Bacteriology
University of Wisconsin
Madison, Wisconsin

MANURE

POOP

DUNG DOO-DOO

PUBLISHING

New York, New York

Credits

Cover, © efendy/Shutterstock; 4, © Toby Houlton/Alamy; 5, © Cyril Ruoso/Biosphoto; 6, © Atovot/iStock Photo; 7, © Ruth Owen Books; 7TL, © TigerOmg/Shutterstock; 7TR, © Esther van Praag; 7BL, © Kizel Cotiw-an/Shutterstock; 7BR, © KanphotoSS/Shutterstock; 8T, © Dave Watts/Alamy; 8B, © OlegD/Shutterstock; 9, © Dave Watts/Alamy; 10T, © SCIMAT/Science Photo Library; 11, © Grobler du Preez/Alamy; 12, © nattanan726/Shutterstock; 13, © Barbara Dobner/Friends of the Koala; 14T, © NagyDodo/Shutterstock; 14B, © Henrik Larsson/Shutterstock; 15, © efendy/Shutterstock; 16, © Martin Maritz/Shutterstock; 17, © Jan Mastnik/Shutterstock; 18, © John Michael Evan Potter/Shutterstock; 19TR, © Scott Hurd/Alamy; 19, © NSP-RF/Alamy; 20, © D.P. Wilson/FLPA; 21, © Tony Wu/Nature Picture Library; 22L, © kamomeen/Shutterstock; 22R, © Ruth Owen Books; 23TL, © Tischenko Irina/Shutterstock; 23TC, © Albie Venter/Shutterstock; 23TR, © Ruth Owen Books; 23BL, © Jan Mastnik/Shutterstock; 23BC, © John Michael Evan Potter/Shutterstock; 23BR, © photofort 77/Shutterstock.

Publisher: Kenn Goin
Senior Editor: Joyce Tavolacci
Creative Director: Spencer Brinker
Photo Researcher: Ruth Owen Books

Library of Congress Cataloging-in-Publication Data

Names: Lawrence, Ellen, 1967– author.
Title: Poop eaters / by Ellen Lawrence.
Description: New York, New York : Bearport Publishing, [2018] | Series: The
   scoop on poop | Audience: Ages 5–8. | Includes bibliographical references
   and index.
Identifiers: LCCN 2017014720 (print) | LCCN 2017019439 (ebook) |
   ISBN 9781684022984 (ebook) | ISBN 9781684022441 (library)
Subjects: LCSH: Animal droppings—Juvenile literature. |
   Animals—Food—Juvenile literature. | Animal behavior—Juvenile literature.
Classification: LCC QL768 (ebook) | LCC QL768 .L2925 2018 (print) | DDC
   591.5—dc23
LC record available at https://lccn.loc.gov/2017014720

For more information, write to Bearport Publishing Company, Inc., 45 West 21st Street, Suite 3B, New York, New York 10010. Printed in the United States of America.

10 9 8 7 6 5 4 3 2 1

Contents

What's for Dinner?

A rabbit is nibbling on grass and wildflowers.

Then the furry little animal tucks its head between its legs.

It gobbles up soft, moist balls of poop coming out of its own backside!

Gross—or is it?

As strange as it seems, rabbits need to eat their own poop to stay healthy.

a rabbit eating its own poop

guinea pig

It's not just rabbits that eat their own waste. Guinea pigs, chinchillas, hamsters, and many other animals are poop eaters, too!

How exactly do you think a rabbit benefits from eating its own poop?

Time to Eat—Twice!

A rabbit gets the **nutrients** it needs from food—and from its own poop!

After it eats, the rabbit's meal enters a part of its **digestive system** called the cecum.

Here, the food becomes a special, nutritious poop called cecotropes.

The rabbit poops out the squishy, greenish-brown cecotropes and eats them.

Then the cecotropes pass back through the rabbit's digestive system.

After the cecotropes pass back through the rabbit's digestive system, they are pooped out as dry, brown fecal pellets.

Rabbit Digestion

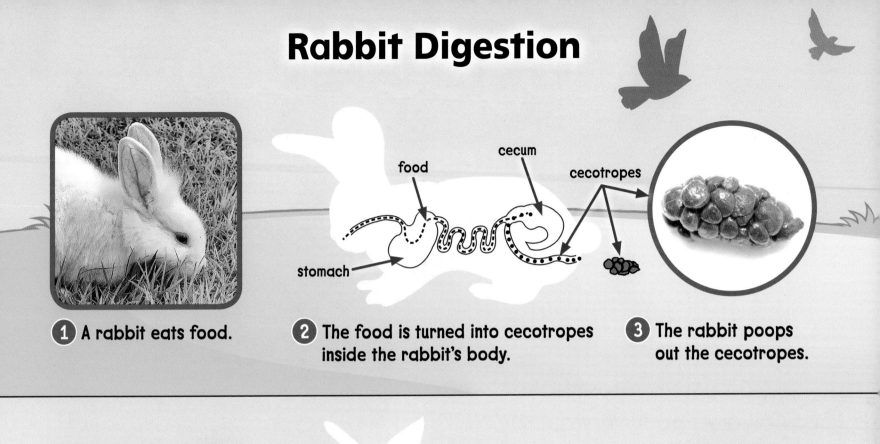

food

cecum

cecotropes

stomach

1 A rabbit eats food.

2 The food is turned into cecotropes inside the rabbit's body.

3 The rabbit poops out the cecotropes.

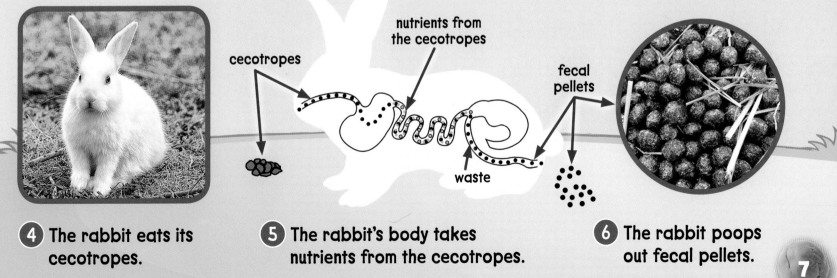

cecotropes

nutrients from the cecotropes

fecal pellets

waste

4 The rabbit eats its cecotropes.

5 The rabbit's body takes nutrients from the cecotropes.

6 The rabbit poops out fecal pellets.

Fruity Doo-Doo

In the forests of New Guinea lives another poop-eating animal called the cassowary.

This huge bird gobbles down lots of fruit.

The fruit passes through the cassowary's body very quickly.

To get enough nutrients, the bird eats its own fruity poop!

That way, the nutritious fruit goes through its digestive system a second time.

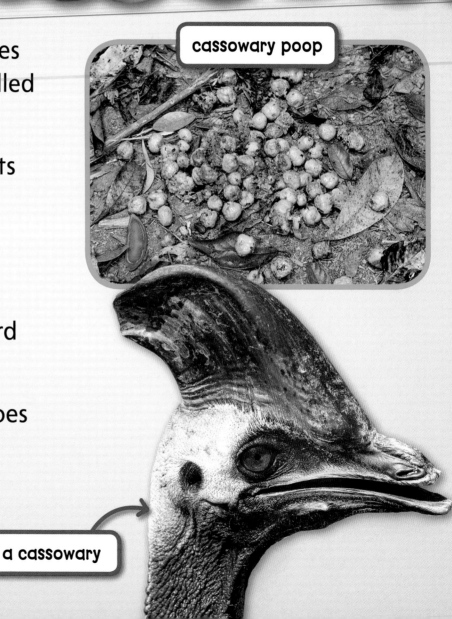

cassowary poop

a cassowary

father cassowary

Cassowary chicks are raised by their fathers. The little birds often feed on their dad's mushy poop to get the nutrients they need.

chick

Poo from Parents

Some young animals eat their parents' poop. Why?

It's good for their digestive systems.

Inside an animal's stomach are millions of tiny **bacteria** that help digest food.

These bacteria also live in feces.

Often, baby animals are born without these helpful bacteria.

By eating mom or dad's poop, they get some of the bacteria they need to be healthy.

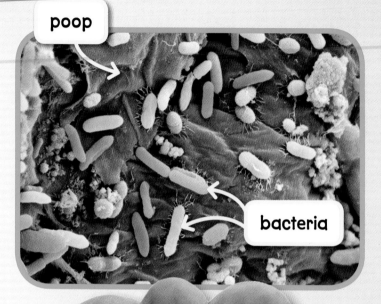

poop

bacteria

When young elephant and rhino calves are ready to eat solid food, their first meal is often mom's dung. The dung contains bacteria that will help them digest the grass and other plants they'll eventually eat.

mother elephant

calf

dung

11

Protection from Poison

A mother koala's poop is an essential meal for a baby koala.

Adult koalas feed on poisonous gum tree leaves.

The animals don't get sick, however, because their guts contain bacteria that break down the poison.

Baby koalas, or joeys, eat their mother's poop to take in the special bacteria.

This prepares their bodies for a diet of poisonous leaves!

A mother koala produces a runny, greenish-brown poop called pap for her joey to eat. The baby licks the pap from its mother's body.

pap

mother koala

gum tree leaves

joey

13

Soupy Poop

Not all poop eaters feast on their own waste or their parents'.

Some, such as dung beetles, feed on their neighbors' poop!

Whether it's elephant or cattle dung—it's all food to a hungry dung beetle.

The beetles slurp up the smelly liquid that's found in a fresh pile of dung.

They get all the water and nutrition they need from the wet, poopy pile!

dung beetles on poop

a dung beetle feeding

There are more than 6,000 different types of dung beetles. Some dung beetles roll dung into balls.

How do you think parent dung beetles use poop to care for their babies?

On a Roll!

Dung beetles that roll poop into balls are known as rollers.

When it's time to **mate**, a pair of rollers works as a team to make and bury dung balls.

Then, after mating, the female beetle lays an egg in each one.

Soon after, a fat, white **larva** hatches from each egg.

Then the larva feeds on the poop ball prepared by its parents.

a pair of roller beetles at work

The poop balls that dung beetles bury are full of nutrients. When the balls break down, these nutrients get mixed into the soil and help plants grow.

dung beetle larva

dung ball

A Stool Snack

In Africa, leopard tortoises have an unusual relationship with hyenas.

The tortoises eat plants that don't have a lot of **calcium**.

One way the tortoises can get calcium is by gnawing on animal bones.

However, they've found an easier way to get the nutrients they need.

They eat hyena poop, which contains crushed bone and loads of calcium!

hyena

elephant leg bone

Hyenas feed on wildebeest, antelopes, elephants, and other animals. Their powerful jaws help them crunch up every bit of an animal, including its bones.

leopard tortoise

hyena poop

Whales make a huge amount of poop. In what ways do you think it might be good for the ocean?

Whale Waste

When a whale poops, it creates an enormous cloud of waste— and a huge feast!

Tiny ocean plants called phytoplankton feed on the nutrients in whale poop.

The phytoplankton are then eaten by small animals called zooplankton.

In turn, the zooplankton become food for shrimp, fish, and other animals.

Whale poop ends up feeding billions of creatures in the ocean!

zooplankton

Whales dive deep underwater to feed on squid and other nutritious foods. Then they poop at the water's surface, helping to spread the nutrients throughout the ocean.

whale poop

sperm whale

21

Science Lab

Poop Food Chains

Whale poop helps spread nutrients on land, too. How?

1. Fish feed on whale poop.

2. Seabirds eat the fish and then poop on land. Some fish, such as salmon, swim up rivers and are eaten by bears.

3. When the birds and bears poop, they spread nutrients that help trees and other plants grow.

Use colored pencils to draw a picture of a food chain that shows how whale poop becomes food for living things in the ocean and on land.

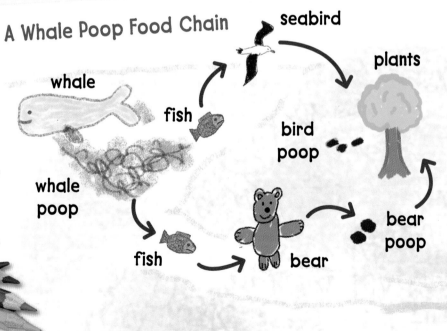

A Whale Poop Food Chain

whale

fish

whale poop

fish

bear

bear poop

plants

bird poop

seabird

Science Words

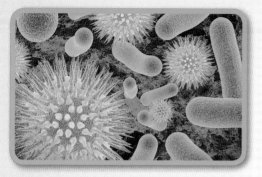

bacteria (bac-TEER-ee-uh) tiny living things; some are helpful while others cause disease

calcium (KAL-see-uhm) a type of nutrient that helps keep an animal's bones and teeth strong and healthy

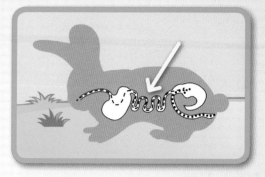

digestive system (dye-JESS-tiv SISS-tuhm) the organs inside a body that help break down food

larva (LAR-vuh) a young insect that has a fat, wormlike body

mate (MAYT) to come together to have young

nutrients (NOO-tree-uhnts) substances that are found in food and are needed by living things to stay healthy

Index

Read More

Johnson, Rebecca. *Danny the Dung Beetle (Bug Adventures).* New York: Rosen (2016).

Owen, Ruth. *Horrible Animal Habits (It's A Fact!).* New York: Ruby Tuesday (2014).

Rake, Jody S. *Why Rabbits Eat Poop and Other Gross Facts About Pets.* North Mankato, MN: Capstone (2012).

Learn More Online

To learn more about poop eaters, visit **www.bearportpublishing.com/TheScoopOnPoop**

About the Author

Ellen Lawrence lives in the United Kingdom. Her favorite books to write are those about nature and animals. In fact, the first book Ellen bought for herself when she was six years old was the story of a gorilla named Patty Cake that was born in New York's Central Park Zoo.